101 QUOTES THAT WILL CHANGE THE WAY YOU THINK

BRIANNA WIEST

THOUGHT
CATALOG
Books

THOUGHTCATALOG.COM

THOUGHT CATALOG Books

Published by Thought Catalog Books, an imprint of Thought Catalog, a digital magazine owned and operated by The Thought & Expression Co. Inc., an independent media organization founded in 2010 and based in the United States of America. For stocking inquiries, contact stockists@shopcatalog.com.

Produced by Chris Lavergne and Noelle Beams
Art direction and design by KJ Parish
Circulation management by Isidoros Karamitopoulos

thoughtcatalog.com | shopcatalog.com

This book is set in Orpheus, designed by Walter Tiemann in 1928.
First Edition, Limited Edition Pressing
Printed in the United States of America

ISBN 978-1-949759-83-9

The most miraculous things in our lives are the ones that change how we see things, each other, and ourselves. It's the relinquishing that hope is not lost, for there is another way that life can be.

Your body will never choose loss
So, instead of focusing on
how much less you want
Weight, fights, debt, worry
Focus on what more you want
Strength, harmony, freedom, certainty
It is in building the new that we are freed
Not in damning the old

You won't get over what's really meant for you. You will only ever become more and more aware that you're denying yourself the greatest joy in fear of the possibly greatest disappointment. I can't believe I'm throwing this quote in here, but I can't think of anything that sums it up better:

> *The brave may not live forever,*
> *but the cautious don't live at all.*

Your mountain is the block between you and the life you want to live. Facing it is also the only path to your freedom and becoming. You are here because a trigger showed you to your wound, and your wound will show you to your path, and your path will show you to your destiny.

In many ways, the journey of healing is not so much a chapter in your story but changing the way you write the entire book. It's a shift in the way you move through the world, one in which you move from being disappointed that life has not met your every expectation to expanding your vision to perceive all of the magic, the wonder, the awe, the heartache, the loss, the gain, the contrast that makes us all perfectly and unpredictably human.

I hope you find the courage to change your life. In the small ways, in the big ways, in every way that matters. I hope you do not end this story with a heart full of regrets. I hope you do not spend your years just waiting for your life to begin. I hope you realize that this is not the practice run, this is not the preview. This is it. There is nothing to do but leap. There is nothing to do but allow yourself to exist as boldly and honestly as you can. You are not waiting on another person, or the right timing, or for everything to fall into place. You are waiting to feel ready enough to exist within the questions, to not need every answer, and to know that this life does not come to us to be perfectly understood, but to be fully experienced.

Make your life a safe haven in which only people who have the capacity to care and listen and connect are allowed.

The person you become when you are on your own is a garden you will carry with you forever. Use the quiet. Even if every single thing in your life works out exactly the way you want it to, you wake up with yourself every day. You have to know who you want to be.

BRIANNA WIEST

The deepest form of self-care is building a life you are in love with, and that is often a very unbeautiful thing. It means making a spreadsheet of your debt and enforcing a morning routine and cooking yourself healthy meals and no longer running from your problems and calling the distraction a solution. It means looking your failures and disappointments square in the eye and restrategizing. It is not satiating your immediate desires. It is letting go. It is choosing new. It is disappointing some people. It is making sacrifices for others. It is living in a way other people won't, so maybe you can live in a way other people can't. It is becoming the person you know you want and are meant to be. Someone who knows that salt baths and chocolate cake are ways to enjoy life—not escape from it.

One day, the mountain that is in front of you will be so far behind you, it will barely be visible in the distance. But the person you become in learning to get over it? That will stay with you forever—and that is the point of the mountain.

All you will regret
is not reaching
harder for the
things you actually
wanted while
they were still in
front of you.

Forget all that. All you planned and all you expected, all you anticipated life to be. All the stories you tell yourself about who you are and what you're capable of. What if the limit is solely within your mind? What if the callings in your heart are a better and clearer measure of what's truly possible? What if, all along, what you needed was the courage to feel, to know, and to leap? There is love and there is potential and there is beauty flowing from every moment of your life. Yes, even right here, and even right now. The world does not change, your perception changes. You sensitize yourself to what was there all along. So I hope you will allow your life to be bigger than you ever thought it could be. I hope you will wipe the mental slate clean and begin again, with the truth of who you are today, and all you hope to be tomorrow. I hope you will realize just how much is within you and around you. I hope you will let yourself do more than you ever thought you could.

You're never as fixated on how you appear as when you don't like how you feel. You're never as concerned about whether or not other people like you as when you quietly dislike yourself. You are never as worried about what's outside of your control as when you're not acting on all that is within it. You're never seeking other people's approval more than when you do not feel you've made the right decisions. There is nobody else you need to convince that you are enough for your own life–you have to alter the way you live it so that it actually feels like enough for you. The happier you are with your life, the less you need other people to be.

I hope this is the year you change your life. Not in the superficial way. Not in the way of moving things around on the surface and wondering why nothing feels much different underneath. Not in the way of conformity. Not in the way that aligns you most closely with all of the traditional emblems of success, the ones that leave you smiling beside your accomplishments but feeling so pinched with regret. I hope this is the year you change your life in all the ways you have always secretly wanted to. The year you discover those quiet dreams that have lingered for so long are actually echoes of parallel lives, sister stories asking you to tell them, to leap toward them, to move them out of your mind and into a touchable, physical reality.

You may not see it today or tomorrow, but eventually all of the pieces will add up and bring you somewhere wonderful, or where you always wanted to be. You will be grateful that some things did not work out the way you once wanted them to.

Everything heals
and grows when
it is loved well.
People, too.

A mind-blowing,
singular breakthrough is not
what changes your life.
A microshift is.

You may believe that living life to the fullest is seeing every country in the world and quitting your job on a whim and falling recklessly in love, but it's really just knowing how to be where your feet are. It's learning how to take care of yourself, how to make a home within your own skin. It's learning how to build a simple life you are proud of. A life most fully lived is not always composed of the things that rock you awake, but those that slowly assure you it's okay to slow down. That you don't always have to prove yourself. That you don't need to fight forever, or constantly want more. That it's okay for things to be just as they are. Little by little, you will begin to see that life can only grow outward in proportion to how stable it is inward; that if the joy is not in the little things first, the big things won't fully find us.

When you do not
know what is next,
you enter the realm
of infinite potential.

What if there is a path for you that is greater than what you can envision? What if there is a life for you that is more than you would even know to ask for? What if you are inherently and unknowingly limited by your old perspectives, your outdated ideas of what is possible? What if all the discomfort within your being is simply trying to redirect you to a place beyond anything you've considered before? What if there is more than you know? What if there are things out there so good you don't even know you're waiting for them?

One day, you will realize that true success is not the way things look, but how they feel— and a life that feels truly good will require you to be uncomfortable. It will ask you to stretch. It will force you to be vulnerable, to lay your heart bare. It will prompt you to make the hardest choices and to reconcile the fact that sometimes, what's hard is also what's right. It will force you into integrity. It will open you where you've tried to build every wall. It will make you process every hurt you thought you had moved beyond, only to discover it had been lingering somewhere inside, waiting to be felt, to be held.

Maybe you feel stuck because you have tried to force stillness when what you really need is to keep going. Maybe you're tired not because your body is depleted but because your soul needs to be nourished. Maybe you're alone because what you most need to learn about yourself can only be learned in solitude. Maybe you don't feel good enough because you have not yet allowed someone into the places where you feel most unworthy and let them love you there. Maybe it's quiet because you need to hear the sound of your own voice. Maybe you feel lost because you're getting a chance to choose something greater than what you once assumed the best could be.

What's truly right for you will inspire you as much as it terrifies you. What's truly right for you will feel like a complete unknown and a homecoming, all at once. What's truly right for you will feel like a victory lap and an exhale—as though you are reaching beyond anything you've ever believed yourself capable of doing, and yet finally returning to what you've always known was yours.

Each day, your mind is met with quiet, inspired ideas–nudges, inklings, wonderings. These are the pathways to your own self-actualization. Each time you let one slip away, you are deciding to stay right where you are. The shift is subtle: when you feel the push, go there. Call that person, change that space, create that thing. Opportunity only lives in the moment. You remain beneath your potential each day you leave your potential on the table. Start picking it up.

Just because you can feel every burden does not mean that they are all yours to carry.

One day, there will be a dream planted in your heart that seems beyond your capacity to hold, beyond your ability to manifest. That is when the journey of your life will begin. The journey into trust, into surrender, into releasing the old and embracing the new. I hope you will begin to see the space between where you are and where you want to be not as one of lack or impossibility, but as an opportunity to gently build the person you want to be into form. Realizing, at last, that what we are asking life to give us is what life is waiting for us to give it. When we want love, our task is to be more loving. When we want change, our task is to be more daring. When we want progress, our task is to be more organized. When we want awe, our task is to be more grateful.

What is meant for you will arrive in your life and it will remain in your life. What did not transpire was not meant to; the end of that journey would not have led you somewhere you would have wanted or needed to be. If you are really honest with yourself, you know this on the inside. There were so many signs that you willingly brushed over in the heat of blind hope. If you spend your life fixated on the might-have-beens, you miss out on the steady currents that have carried you all this way. Notice what stays. Notice what is constant. Notice what perseveres. These are the things that the song of your life will be composed of.

You must learn to let your conscious decisions dictate your day–not your fears or impulses.

If you would like to change your life, you must first change the way you think about your life. Thoughts are not just thoughts. They are bridges and doors and entryways and foundations. They magnetize and repel. They can build a house and tear it down. They can energize momentum or keep you idling within your own little world forever. Thoughts are investments, and they are decisions. The mind will generate an endless series of options—some inspiring, and others terrifying—and so you must choose. You must choose what you will return to, what you will believe in, what you will place weight on. Because thoughts create feeling, and feeling creates desire, and desire creates action, and action creates reward, and reward creates more desire, and before you know it, a thought became a torch that led you down the path that is your life. If you would like to change your life, you must first change the way you think about your life. There was never another way.

Healing is not about going back to exactly who you were before, because that person was not capable of seeing the storm before it hit, and that person didn't know how to shield themselves from it. You aren't supposed to go back to being more naive or unaware. You aren't meant to return to your mindlessness, a life in which you didn't know the contrasts. What you get through healing is greater than a return, it is a rebirth. You become stronger where you've been broken. You become grounded where you've been egotistical. You become responsible where you've been neglectful. You become more sensitive and conscious. You become more considerate, more empathetic, more mindful, more careful. You learn the hard lessons so you can open your heart to the lighter ones. You come more fully into the experience of being alive.

Self-protection is learning how to take a pause between what you feel and how you react. When there is no awareness between what you perceive and the way that you respond, anything can control you. Practice the pause. Widen the space between what you sense and what you do about it. Decide what's worth your energy, because what you engage with is what you empower.

What you are waiting on is your own willingness to accept the mountain you must climb in order to pull those desires out of the deepest parts of you and create them in the world you already inhabit.

Productivity is how you run away from yourself
Creativity is how you become yourself

One day, you will look back on this time, and all you will see is magic.

Love them where they are. If someone is falling behind in life, you don't have to remind them. They already know. If someone is unhealthy, they know. If someone is struggling with relationships, with money, with self-image...they know. It's what consumes their thoughts each day. What you need to do for those who are in that place is not to reprimand but to encourage. To tell them what's good about their lives, to show them the potential within them that you see. What you need to do is love them where they are. When we can't see clearly for ourselves, we need others to speak greatness over us. People don't need you to tell them what's wrong with their lives—they already know. They need you to reassure them that they can still make it right.

What you believe about your life is what you will make true about your life.

Almost when you least expect it, things fall into place. You realize that what left was making space for what was about to arrive. The quiet let you hear the guidance. The unhappiness forced you to make a move. The unsettledness made you keep seeking. The end ushered in a new beginning. The doors that closed turned you toward the ones that were opening. The lessons were always leading you. Every time you got it wrong, you came one step closer to having it right. You began to realize that the person you are is the aperture through which you experience everything, and the growth was always about refining that person to better respond to what is heavy, and appreciate what is light.

A beautiful life is not stumbled upon, it is built. It is chosen. It is nurtured over the years. A beautiful life is made from the heart, not the head. It is not one we can rationalize our way into, it's one that must be felt. A beautiful life is not one that is immediately comfortable, but one grown through the acknowledgment of what is worth being uncomfortable for. It is not one that is easy, it is one that is worth it.

The little things—the long baths, the page-turning novels, the quiet Saturday mornings, the stars, the ocean, the city lights—they were the big things all along.

Life is subjective, temporary, and fleeting, sometimes terribly painful but also extraordinarily beautiful...all at the same time.

Free yourself from the confines that bind you. Maybe you built steel bars around your heart because you thought they had to be there. You wanted to protect yourself from being hurt so badly again. Take them down. Walk out. This may be physical, or it may be metaphorical. But either way, know there's nothing worse than not experiencing life for fear of what it may bring.

Life is not a
series of problems
to be solved;
it's a journey that
you should be
fascinated by.

Whenever you feel hopeless, all you need to do is go outside and realize that you have been molded into human form for some reason.

Real change happens in subtle motions
But mostly, it's deciding to create a life
That didn't exist before
And that is the beauty of the
things that break you
They force you to create
yourself anew to move on
And perhaps that was the point
All along

I hope you allow your life to be bigger than you ever thought it could be. I hope you allow yourself to embody more beauty than you ever thought possible. I hope you don't get trapped by the small stories, the little ideas you had about what the future may be. I hope you don't long for the things you've outgrown just because they're familiar. I hope you don't consider everything you lose to be a loss. I hope you don't define yourself only by the limits of what you've known. I hope you do not cap your potential at what others have said is possible. Most of all, I hope you recognize the light when it hits you. I hope you let yourself do more than you ever thought you could.

Everything that is truly right for you will make you feel at peace. Everything that is meant for you will feel like a deep exhale, as though you are returning home to a place you forgot existed. We so often reach for the things that help us escape who we are, but the things that are actually meant for us–the ones that arrive and stay–they make us feel a sense of steady calm. We do not need to be swept off our feet, but grounded through them.

The most precious, important thing that you have in your life is your energy. It is not your time that is limited; it is your energy. What you give it to each day is what you will create more and more of in your life. What you give your time to is what will define your existence.

Not everything you lose is a loss. Some things are a freedom. Some things are a second chance. Some things are a miracle in disguise. Some things are a detachment long-needed, a clarity brought to blurry eyes. Some things are an intervention. Some things are the unexpected answer to a long-chanted prayer. Some things are a healing. Some things are a becoming. Some things are planned long before you ever came to be. Some things are a devastation, but others are a kind of vital guidance, the kind of course-correction you did not even know you needed. The kind you did not even realize you were asking for all along.

When you heal yourself
You heal everyone
When you're reaping a harvest
You can feed everyone
Don't let anyone tell you
That taking care of yourself is selfish
It's the only path
To enlightening the whole

One day you will realize that happiness is
not what your house looks like, but how you
love the people within its walls. Happiness
is not finding success by a certain time, but
finding something you love so much that
time itself seems to disappear. Happiness
is not thinking you have earned the world's
approval, but waking up each day and feeling
so at peace within your own skin, quietly
anticipating the day ahead, unconcerned
with how you are perceived. Happiness is not
having the best of everything, but the ability
to make the best of anything. Happiness
is knowing you are doing what you can
with what you were given. Happiness is not
something that comes to you when every
problem is solved and all things are perfectly
in place, but in the shining silver linings
that remind us the light of day is always
there, if you slow down enough to notice.

Accomplishing goals is not success.

How much you expand in the process is.

We don't need a lot to be happy, but we do need things that are real. We do need things that grip our hearts and enliven us and make us feel like we are here for a reason, here to experience something that could only be touched by a human body, understood by a human mind, loved by a human heart. When we deny ourselves the authentic experience of being alive, we reach for more when what we really want is not to stretch wider, but to go deeper.

The journey is not about knowing what the right thing to do is, but finding the courage to do it. Convincing your mind to act consistently on what your heart already knows. No longer starting wars on the inside to keep the peace on the outside. Not prioritizing the people who only consider you an option. Not taking the advice of anyone you wouldn't want to switch places with. Declining what doesn't feel right. Accepting what does. Speaking truth where you once could only hold your breath and endure the pressure of holding it just beneath your heart. Taking quiet when you need quiet, and movement when you need change. Trying, again and again, until you arrive somewhere you can be proud of, that you can make peace with. Until your efforts are moving in the direction of your most honest desires. Until the person you are on the outside begins to match the one living within.

The people, places, and things that are destined for you are the ones that give you as much energy as they take. What's meant for us becomes a symbiotic force; when we move toward what's right, what's right moves toward us.

If you ever get the chance, go alone. Walk alone, travel alone, live alone, dance alone. Just for a while. If you ever get the chance, learn who you are when the world isn't demanding you be one way or another. Most people only know how to stand on their own if someone else will stand beside them. Don't let that be your story. When you get the chance, know that the opportunity to walk alone, even for a bit, is a rare gift, one that will hand you insight that can change the course of your life.

BRIANNA WIEST

Sometimes, you get what you want. Other times, you get a lesson in patience, timing, alignment, empathy, compassion, faith, perseverance, resilience, humility, trust, meaning, awareness, resistance, purpose, clarity, grief, beauty, and life. Either way, you win.

You will have to learn that if you are not growing, you are not really living. If you are not moving on from anything, you are not moving toward something. You will have to learn how to let go of some things that are still beautiful, because you know they are not quite right, because you know that a deeper peace is waiting.

Your new life is going to cost you your old one. It's going to cost you your comfort zone and your sense of direction. It's going to cost you relationships and friends. It's going to cost you being liked and understood. It doesn't matter. The people who are meant for you are going to meet you on the other side. You're going to build a new comfort zone around the things that actually move you forward. Instead of being liked, you're going to be loved. Instead of being understood, you're going to be seen. All you're going to lose is what was built for a person you no longer are. Let it go.

In everything you choose, you must first ask, "but what will this do to my soul?" Will it bring me closer to a heavenly state of being or anchor me into the ache of this world? Will it make me more of the person I was meant to be or will it distract me from the true work? Will it pay the bills but bankrupt my being? Will it impress others but disappoint the child inside me waiting to see what I do with my freedom? Will I arrive to the end of my life proud that I did this? Will I choose now or will I wait until I am forced to make the decision I already know is right today? Will I spare myself the suffering? Will I have courage?

You are exactly where you need to be. This is the perfect day to start your life again.

Decide you're deserving of real friendship, true commitment, and complete love with people who are healthy and thriving.

The things you love about others
are the things you love about yourself.
The things you hate about others are
the things you cannot see in yourself.

The things we lose are not losses

They are entryways

They are the world saying, sometimes sharply,

There is something else out there

It is the hardest thing you will ever have to do,
and it will also be the most important: stop giving
your love to those who aren't ready to love you.
Stop having hard conversations with people who
don't want to change. Stop showing up for people
who are indifferent about your presence. Stop
prioritizing people who make you an option.
Stop loving people who aren't ready to love you.

What if, after an entire lifetime of
being sold the idea that the point
of your life is to exist as perfectly
as possible, you could now open
up to the notion that perhaps
you are instead here to enjoy
the ride while you're still on it?

Real growth
requires genuine
exploration, a
period of trial and
error. It requires
you to first admit
that you might
not know what
you want.

The real love story was always you and you. It was how you walked alone and learned what you needed to carry. It was how you began to see through your own eyes and not someone else's. It was how you began to dig joy out from beneath your cynicism, how you slowly built your desires into form. It was how you learned what you like and don't, and what you came here to be. The real love story was always how you opened your heart to yourself.

What feels on the surface like rejection is often redirection. When you ask for a big life, you cannot keep fighting for a smaller one to stay.

Will you continue to replay the memories of yesterday, or will you meet the moment and make the most of what is in front of you now?

What if you knew that you were never meant to get it right the first time, but to build it through trial and error? How much more grace would you give yourself, how much more human might you be?

The point was never that you adjusted everything around you until it was made perfect but that you adjusted the way you see everything until you realize that it is enough, and it always has been.

The reality is that you exist in so many different forms and images and beliefs and stories–and yet, the only one that is ever really going to matter is the one you tell yourself.

It is very hard to show up as the person you want to be when you are surrounded by an environment that makes you feel like a person you aren't.

When we self-sabotage, it is often because we have a negative association between achieving the goal we aspire to and being the kind of person who has or does that thing.

Rock bottom becomes a turning
point because it is only at that
point that most people think:
I never want to feel
this way again.

To truly heal, you are going to have to change the way you think. You are going to have to become very conscious of negative and false beliefs and start shifting to a mindset that actually serves you.

Stop accepting your own excuses.
Stop being complacent with your own
justifications. Start quantifying your days
by how many healthy, positive things
you accomplished, and you will see how
quickly you begin to make progress.

The greatest act of self-love is to no longer accept a life you are unhappy with. It is to be able to state the problem plainly and in a straightforward manner.

Self-sabotage is what happens when we refuse to consciously meet our innermost needs, often because we do not believe we are capable of handling them.

You fall in love with yourself when the child inside looks at the adult you are now and sees the ease of their own approval.

We do not let go by standing within the ruins but by building the life that was trying to emerge all along.

When we ask to greet a new horizon, we have to learn to embrace the journey that will get us there.

You must know what love isn't to know what love is. You must be who you aren't to discover who you are.

You are so busy
standing in your ruins
That you are not
building a new city

If you're meant to go from point A to point B, you will get there eventually. But you can choose which way you go and how you travel.

Your habits create your mood, and your mood is a filter through which you experience your life.

The main thing socially intelligent people understand is that your relationship to everyone else is an extension of your relationship to yourself.

What you have to know is that suffering is just the refusal to accept what is.

Your mind is fire
It can heat your house
Or burn it to the ground

A lack of routine is just a breeding ground for perpetual procrastination.

Everything in your life does one of three
things: shows you to yourself, heals
a part of yourself, or lets you enjoy
a part of yourself. If you adopt that
perspective, there's nothing left to fear.

Getting unstuck is realizing that you were never stuck in the first place; you only stopped to ask yourself, "Is this what I'm here for?"

Everything you've ever dreamed, wanted, worked for, wished for, and are waiting for stems from this moment. What you do now is not just something; it's everything.

Bad feelings should not always be interpreted as deterrents. They are also indicators that you are doing something frightening and worthwhile.

You think your past defines you, and worse, you think that it is an unchangeable reality when, really, your perception of it changes as you do.

People postpone their happiness to keep themselves safe. You cannot save up your happiness; you can either feel it in the moment or you miss it.

Happiness is not how many things you do but how well you do them. More is not better. Happiness is not experiencing something else; it's continually experiencing what you already have in new and different ways.

If you're wondering what you should do with your life, it's likely that you're in the limbo between realizing you don't want what you once did and giving yourself permission to want what you want now.

Everyone fears rejection, but not everyone gets to truly experience the kind of acceptance that comes from being yourself unconditionally.

You're not supposed to be happy all the time. Negative emotions are a signal that something isn't right. The emotion doesn't have to be fixed; the thing that it's signaling your attention to does.

Make plans to build the life you want, not because you hate the one you have, but because you're in love with the person you know you want to become.

All quotations
are excerpts
from the
following books
written by
Brianna Wiest:

101 Essays That Will Change The Way You Think
The Mountain Is You, Ceremony, Salt Water, The Truth About Everything,
When You're Ready, This Is How You Heal, and *The Pivot Year.*

about
the
author

Brianna Wiest is the internationally bestselling author of *101 Essays That Will Change The Way You Think*, *The Mountain Is You*, and more. Her books have sold over 1M copies worldwide, regularly appear on global bestseller lists, and are being translated into more than 40 languages. She lives in California.

briannawiest.com
Instagram.com/briannawiest
Twitter.com/briannawiest
Speaking inquiries: info@briannawiest.com